ALLIS-CHALMERS

ALLIS-CHALMERS
AGRICULTURAL MACHINERY

BILL HUXLEY

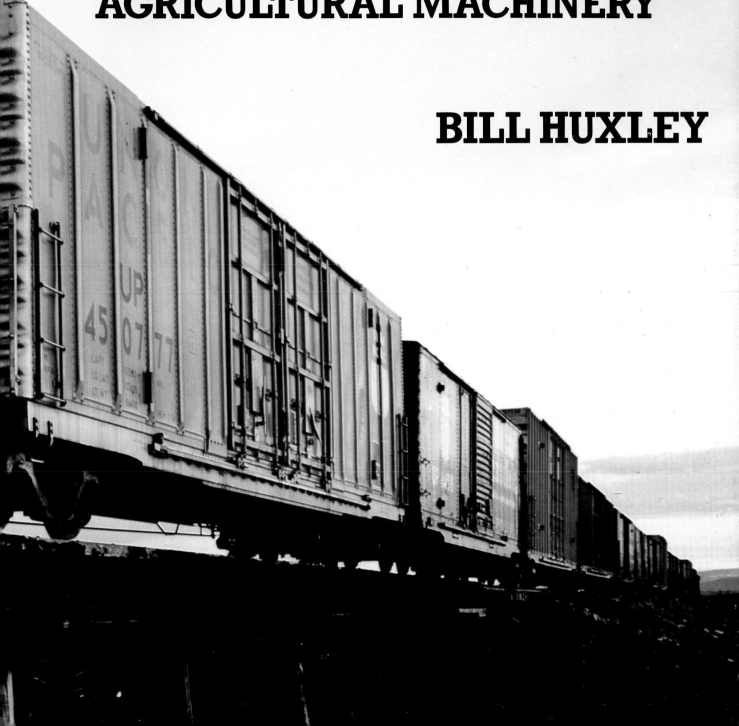

Published in 1988 by Osprey Publishing Limited
59 Grosvenor Street, London W1X 9DA
Reprinted spring 1991

British Library Cataloguing in Publication Data

Huxley, Bill
    Allis-Chalmers: agricultural machinery
    1. Allis-Chalmers tractors, to 1987
    I. Title
    629.2′25
ISBN 0-85045-860-4

Editor Tony Thacker
Design Roger Walker

Filmset by Tameside Filmsetting Limited,
Ashton-under-Lyne, Lancashire
Printed in Hong Kong

Half-title illustration Farmers in the cotton-growing
areas were also catered for, the last model available
being the 880. Shown here is the 860 Cotton Picker.

Title-page illustration The impact of dynamic
advertising of the 1970s. Readers and owners of A-C
equipment may remember this picture from the
Autumn 1978 issue of *Landhandler*, the house
magazine from the makers for the users. Top of the
two-wheel-drive range, this 181 hp 7080 was hitched
to a $\frac{1}{3}$-mile-long train, courtesy of Union Pacific
Railroad, and when told he had moved this 900-ton
load, the driver commented, 'Heck, I was in third
gear!'—his words, not mine!

Front cover illustration The Model WM of 1941. In
1928, A-C acquired the Monarch Tractor Company;
the Model M evolved from the Monarch, using Model U
components.

Back cover illustration A Model B photographed at
the Ham Hill event near Langport, Somerset.

Right This photograph of myself on a model WC of
1936 was taken at the home of my hosts for my 1984
visit: Ed and Janie Westen of Kewaunee, Wisconsin.
On this visit I again called in at West Allis, and then
thanks to Ed and Janie a visit was made to the late
engine plant at Harvey, Illinois. Altogether a very
good trip.

About the author

Bill Huxley has been an avid Allis-Chalmers enthusiast since the early 1970s. He has operated various pieces of A-C equipment for different employers and owns a large collection of A-C models, plus the only full-size 190 Beachmaster in the UK. Although he has published his own efforts in the past, this is his first commissioned work. No doubt there will be more.

Acknowledgements

For greatly valued help with this publication, I would like to say a big 'thank you' to all contributors, including: E. Allman & Company Limited, Banderet Equipment Inc., Carl Borgstrom, Jim Crowe, Deutz-Allis Corporation, Deutz-Fahr UK Limited, Harry Hoving, Stephen Howe, W. Hylands, *Implement & Tractor*, Siam Kamper, KHD AG, Wilhelm Lange, Milwaukee County Historical Society, Andrew Morland, Derek Mountford, National Institute of Agricultural Botany, Andrew Parlour, Mal and Pat Ray, Henry Roskilly, Bert Schoo, Simplicity Manufacturing Company, Brian Steel, Dick Tindall, University of Nebraska, Virgil Vonsoosten, Ken Wickham, Doug Zoerb, and Osprey for publishing.

For further A-C information, subscribe to *Old Allis News*, 10925 Love Road, Bellevue, Michigan 49021, USA, or write to me at 46 Loomer Road, Chesterton, Newcastle-under-Lyme, Staffordshire ST5 7LB, in the UK.

Bill Huxley
Staffordshire, England 1988

I wish they'd talk to an Allis-Chalmers dealer about lift trucks.

Introduction

With the advent of the gasoline-powered farm tractor at the turn of the century, farm mechanization began to take on a new meaning. The traditional methods of horse and steam power were labour intensive, laborious and costly, but for the increased acreage and output anticipated, the tractor was to provide the answer.

However, it takes a major crisis of some kind to bring new ideas and methods into effect, and in 1914 General Otto Falk, President of the recently reorganized Allis-Chalmers Manufacturing Company, having an extensive farming and business background, decided that the rapidly-growing tractor market would provide his company with additional diversity and profitability. Extensive trials with the European 'Austro' rotary cultivator were undertaken, but it was the 10-18, designed and built at the West Allis works, that would become the A-C entry into this important new market.

The machine illustrated below was owned from new by the Buchmayer family of Johnson County, Iowa, until purchased by the Sleichters a few years ago. Following full restoration by Richard Sleichter, it attended many shows and events as a prime exhibit on A-C trade stands, and is now part of their trust collection of little-known A-C tractors. Richard has both a vast knowledge of and a great liking for this brand, and his colossal help with this book has not gone unnoticed by myself. Thanks again, Richard!

The Allis-Chalmers story began in the year 1847, when Edward Phelps Allis (**above**), a 24-year-old New Yorker of Scottish descent, fresh from Union College, Schenectady, arrived in Milwaukee, Wisconsin, eager to face the challenge of the westward spread of industrialization. His activities initially involved leather goods and real estate, and it was not until 1861 that the company as we know it was formed from the defunct Decker & Seville Reliance Company, makers of French burrstones for flour milling and general ironware.

From that moment onwards, the story was one of continued expansion, involving a wide range of products, albeit with the usual quota of pauses and hiccups along the way. New Year's Eve 1868, and the blowing of a steam whistle, heralded the first of more than 6000 steam engines to be built by Allis over the next 30 years or so, and the enrolment of Edwin Reynolds, of Corliss engine fame, gave an early insight into the astute thinking of E. P. Allis.

In the 1870s period, the coming of W. D. Gray to head the flour-milling machinery department, together with G. M. Hinkley for sawmill production, gave the company added impetus with the innovative ideas they brought with them. The triple-expansion pumping engine of 1886, designed and built for the city of Milwaukee, was possibly their most outstanding product of the time.

Twelve years after the death of E. P. Allis, the merger took place between his company and the Chicago-based Fraser & Chalmers Company, plus Gates Ironworks, also of Chicago, and the Dickson Manufacturing Company of Scranton, Pennsylvania, forming the Allis-Chalmers Manufacturing Company in 1901. The product range thus expanded with sugar-making machinery, mining and crushing equipment, and other consumer goods production. Takeovers became the norm, with the addition of the Bullock Electric Manufacturing Company bringing them into yet another field of expanding activities in 1904. Later sales of turbines to the Boulder Dam and Niagara Falls projects, plus crushing equipment to Chile and steam engines to the Central London Railway, were an indication of the growth of the company.

Acquisitions and the innovative spirit continued, and in more recent times the fuel-cell tractor of 1959, involvement with NASA space projects of the 1960s, and ships' diesels of 43,200 shp (which I saw under construction in 1980) are just a few examples of this fine company's work.

These three photographs are of Messrs Falk, Roberts and Merritt. General Otto H. Falk (**top**) was President of the company during the period 1913 to 1932. He was a man of vision, who saw the growing tractor market as an ideal expansionary move and was largely responsible for the creation of the Allis-Chalmers tractor.

W. A. (Bill) Roberts (**centre**) was born to a farming family in Osceola, Missouri, on 25 August 1897. His farm upbringing was followed by a period of high-school and business-college training, plus a spell with a road contractor building some of the first black-top roads in southwest Missouri. He joined A-C in 1924 as a salesman in Witchita, Kansas, and then was their Canadian sales representative until 1928. The next two years saw him in a farm-machinery partnership in Regina, Saskatchewan. On his return to A-C in 1930, he teamed up with Harry Merritt (**bottom**), and the ensuing partnership became legendary. In 1941, he followed Merritt as manager of the Tractor Division, becoming Vice President in 1943. President of the company from 1951–55, Roberts was a man who literally wore himself out in the service of his company.

Cumbersome, costly tractors in the mid-1920s created some stagnation in sales, and H. C. (Harry) Merritt's approach to the situation on becoming manager of the Tractor Division on 1 January 1926 was that of 'Let's roll up the shirt sleeves and have a look-see.' Thanks to his great efforts and ability, A-C tractors and allied equipment were later to build a first-class reputation in many parts of the world.

9

Having decided on the 10-18 design for their entry into the farm tractor market, production got under way in late 1914. Early 1915 sales brochures boldly stated that it was 'the only tractor that has a one-piece, steel heat-treated frame, no rivets to work loose, and will not sag under the heaviest strains.'

This early works picture shows a 10-18 pulling three 14 in. bottoms in North Dakota. The disparity between drawbar and belt hp can be clearly seen with the figures quoted; nevertheless, the claim for 20 acres of ploughing with only 15 gallons of gasoline must have sounded good at the time.

At this time, experiments were being made with the European 'Austro' rotary cultivator, but this was deemed a little before its time. Instead, the 'Tractor Truck' (**above**) was designed, with some ideas coming from the Monarch Tractor Company, but this half-track design would not gain acceptance for more than 20 years. Of the small quantity built, ten went to Russia and the remainder found duties around the West Allis works.

Next to appear was the 6-12 (**right**), the basic idea being to utilize the vast quantity of horse-drawn implements available at the time. A further option was to hook up two machines back-to-back, using forward and reverse gears and providing twice the normal hp. It was also available as a cane tractor model and was used as a prime mover for the Russell and other road graders. Produced from 1918 with Le Roi four-cylinder motors, it was on sale until 1926 at a greatly-reduced price, being one of their less inspiring designs.

The first really successful model from the West Allis works was the 15-30—a December 1918 sales bulletin announced plans to build a new 6-12 and 15-30 along with the 10-18 in a separate, properly-equipped shop with capacity for 30 tractors a day. This photograph shows the assembly shop under the direction of Fred W. Camm, the first manager of the department. A-C advertising of this period was of a

cautious nature and this tractor soon became the 18-30, while in 1921 the Nebraska tests gave it a 20-35 rating at Test 83. In spite of extensive media advertising and new-fangled radio promotions, such as the 'Talking Tractor', narrated in 1922 by Lee Chaffee of Sears & Chaffee Supply Company of Great Bend, Kansas, sales of this basically sound tractor still did not meet expectations.

12

In 1921, in order to keep pace with the improvements in styling and performance that were beginning to appear, A-C introduced the 12-20 tractor, which was of two/three plough capacity and had a Midwest motor of $4 \times 5\frac{1}{4}$ in. bore and stroke, plus valve-in-head layout. Following tests at Nebraska, it became the 15-25—approximately 1705 units were built by 1927. This is another nice example from the Sleichter trust collection.

The turning point in the fortunes of the tractor department came on 1 January 1926, with the appointment of Harry Merritt as its manager. This 'human tornado' literally tore apart a production model of the unwieldy, overpriced 20-35, and by removing unnecessary items and buying in components where cost-effective, he produced a much lighter, snappier and less-costly machine. From this time onwards, his design and development expertise, later added to Bill Roberts' sales efforts, would bring about a vast upturn in tractor and implement production in the 1930s. Shown below is a recently-restored, later-type 20-35 in the ownership of Pat and Barry Bruce of the Scotbury collection, near Cambridge in the UK.

In 1928, the news that a famous tractor and automobile builder was quitting the US tractor market prompted a group of companies to form the United Tractor & Implement Company, based in Chicago, which led to a 'United' tractor being built by Allis-Chalmers.

As is generally known, the consortium soon folded, but the tractor stayed with A-C as the celebrated Model U, which in its early years was equipped with a Continental L-head motor (side-valve) of $4\frac{1}{4} \times 5$ in. bore and stroke. Early on, hard-rubber-tyred and tracked versions (from the Trackson Company) were offered, and when skid units became available it was then ideally suited for a wide range of agricultural and industrial applications. The U engine and other tractor engines were to be offered as power units for many types of application.

The year 1928 again brought additional models and expansion for A-C with the takeover, in April, of the Monarch Tractor Company, originally of Watertown, Wisconsin. Owing to a series of ownership changes, they had by this time relocated to Springfield, Illinois, and were offering two well-known models of track-type tractor—the Monarch 50 and 75. These would soon be joined by the Monarch 35 which, in 1933, became the K, with the KO heavy oil/diesel version to follow.

17

A low seat for the driver—dust plates to protect him from rising dust—disc wheels and guards—these are among the features of the Allis-Chalmers orchard tractor.

Allis-Chalmers orchard plows are low and narrow to give the greatest possible clearance. They are made by one of the world's leading manufacturers.

The Allis-Chalmers

Is a Powerful . . . Speedy . . . Convenient . . . Economical Orchard Tractor

EXTRA power comes in mighty handy for orchard work — just as it does for field work.

The Allis-Chalmers orchard tractor pulls a 3-bottom moldboard plow, a 10-foot tandem disc or any implement of similar draft.

That extra power saves time and worry when you've a job that must be done FAST. It saves you money, too, for Allis-Chalmers power is notably low in cost.

That same power makes the Allis-Chalmers a great field tractor in between orchard jobs—an all-around tractor for every purpose.

The Allis-Chalmers orchard tractor is built low and compact to pull tillage tools under low limbs. It has plenty of power to take a heavily loaded sprayer up steep slopes — it operates the sprayer through its power takeoff. Whatever the job — EXTRA POWER makes it easier with an Allis-Chalmers.

ALLIS-CHALMERS
TRACTOR DIVISION—MILWAUKEE, U. S. A.

Left By the late 1920s, farmers were becoming able to use a form of 'one-stop shopping' whereby tractor builders offered a range of implements to suit their tractors, thus simplifying the farmer's task in selecting the correct machinery and at the same time adding to company profitability. With this aim in mind, General Falk went shopping in 1929 and returned with the La Crosse Plow Company. Albert Herscheimer, who hailed from Blairsville, Pennsylvania, had bought out the original Barclay & Banton Company in 1865, giving it the title of the La Crosse Plow Works until it assumed the later title in 1893. From this time onwards, 'La Crosse Made' tall tillage implements built up a fine reputation—the purchase of this company, therefore, with its ploughs, discs, drills and other items, proved to be a very astute move by Falk. With the later La Porte takeover, a full range of tillage equipment was on offer to suit the U, 25-40, UC and K tractors. Incidentally, the whistle that Herscheimer used on his steamboat *Eclipse* prior to the buy-out of Barclay & Banton was still located at the works in 1938.

Below Further upgrading took place, with the 20-35 becoming the 25-40, or Model E as it is sometimes known—1000 rpm, $4\frac{3}{4}$ or $5 \times 6\frac{1}{2}$ in. bore and stroke, or $5\frac{1}{4}$ in. bore on the 'Thresherman's Special'. By this time, multispeed transmissions were becoming a necessity and the two fwds on this model would not have been a good sales feature in spite of its power and durability. This machine was phased out in 1936 by the Model A.

On this side of the Atlantic, the 25-40 is a rare beast and this recent acquisition by Stan Robert of Ellesmere, Shropshire, will be a welcome addition at local events.

Following the purchase of the La Crosse Plow Company, A-C were soon to offer crop farmers a means of speeding up their tillage operations with the UC tractor (from 1933 known as the 'All-Crop' tractor). Basically a U with tricycle-type front end and modified rear end, the drive in tool frame could be attached in five minutes. It adopted the UM engine (as with the U) and was built until 1941, with many of the 5000 produced going to the Thompson Cane Equipment Company of Thibodaux, Louisiana. The photograph below shows another nice example from Barry Bruce.

THRESH YOUR OWN
with the
A-C RUMELY
22 x 36 THRESHER

Here's the ideal machine for the man who wants to thresh his own crop, or for the neighborhood ring.

Simple and efficient, it has all of the features and requirements of the larger and more expensive machines, all of the grain saving and grain cleaning qualities as well.

This machine has established an enviable reputation for fast, clean work, and is known wherever grain is grown.

Come in and let us explain its many exclusive features and its *EXTREMELY low price.*

(Dealer's Name and Address Here)

ALLIS·CHALMERS
TRACTOR DIVISION—MILWAUKEE, U. S. A.

Meinhard Rumely is not a name easily remembered outside farming and preservation circles, but to farmers of the period 1852–1931 it meant a range of quality products, such as steam traction engines, separators, threshers and the renowned 'OilPull' tractor, so popular with old tractor buffs. When A-C took over the Rumely company in 1931, several other well-known brand names had been absorbed,

including Gaar-Scott, the Advance Thresher Company, the Northwest Thresher Company and the Aultman-Taylor Company, all of which, together with their extensive dealer network, greatly improved Allis-Chalmers' sales territories, not to mention overseas outlets. The Birdsell Manufacturing Company of South Bend, Indiana, makers of Clover hullers, was also acquired at this time. Illustrated below is the 'DoAll' in cultivator form, which could also be operated as a conventional four-wheeled tractor, owned by Carl Borgstrom of Dousman, Wisconsin, together with a 22 × 36 thresher advertisement (**far left**) from a 1932 sales catalogue.

These are excellent examples of two OilPull models.
Several Rumely products were still on offer until
1935–36 as dealer-stock sell-out items.

The Firestone exhibit at the Century of Progress Exposition, Chicago 1933. The tractor industry needed a boost in the early 1930s—Allis-Chalmers provided it when they pioneered the use of low-pressure air tyres on farm tractors, very simple but very effective. The Model U tractor on display, with matching HTP 314 three-bottom plough, is a demonstration model as it is an earlier Continental-powered version. This engine was superseded at serial number 7404 in 1932 by the Waukesha Motor-built and A-C-designed UM $4\frac{3}{8} \times 5$ in. valve-in-head (ohv) motor.

Travelling at 60 mph in an automobile in 1903 must have been something of a hair-raising experience, not to mention quite an achievement—but that is exactly what Barney Oldfield, ex-Ohio farm boy and wildcat bicycle rider, did in Ford's specially-built 999 racer. Thirty years on, the first man to top one mile a minute in an auto also became the first man to achieve this honour with a farm tractor at Dallas, Texas, on 17 October 1933, when he drove a Model U at 64.28 mph. This record, though, was later topped by Ab Jenkins, who had also driven the same tractor at 35.44 mph around the West Allis stadium track, having just ploughed the infield at a sedate 5 mph! Other feats performed at around this time included driving the almost-90 miles to Chicago in less than five hours and waving speed tickets to the crowds—the same stunt tried today would not receive quite the same reception!

In order to demonstrate the exceptional performance of air-tired tractors, they were demonstrated and raced by famous drivers at state fairs.

Don Prior of Histon, Cambridgeshire, can feel justly proud of his WM (wide-tread) Model M track-type tractor, which looks good and runs well, too. My small contribution was to supply the cap and decals—all the rest is down to Don. The M, WM and orchard M were produced from 1933 to 1942, proving extremely popular in agricultural and construction work owing to the wide range of attachments available. Being based on the U, it shared the same reputation for reliability and performance, and was very popular in the UK as well as in the USA.

Without doubt, one of the most successful tractors from A-C was the WC. The 28 built in 1933 were designated Model W, the official launch being held in 1934, with a total of 178,202 units being built to 1948. The 4 × 4 in. engine was frame mounted as opposed to the usual unitary construction, and was designed for use with drive in mid/rear-mounted tool frames or the mid-mounted mower, which, together with an option of three- or four-wheel front end, several sizes of steel or air-tyred wheels and the

power to operate the All-Crop 60 harvester, made for a really useful mid-range tractor. Further variants for highway maintenance were available from La Porte and were designated W Patrol and WC Speed Maintainer, styled from serial number 74329. This was also the first tractor to be tested at Nebraska with air tyres as a standard fitment. The example shown above belongs to Banderet Equipment Inc., Commerce City, Colorado.

During the early 1930s, an entirely new concept in harvesting underwent development by A-C designers and engineers, which, upon its public trials in 1935, took the farming world by storm. This was the All-Crop 60 trailed-type combine harvester, also known as the 'Cornbelt Combine' and the 'successor to the binder'. Without doubt, this machine infinitely eased the life of the small farmer who previously had harvested with the binder 'reaper' and thresher, a laborious and not altogether profitable procedure. The sum of $495 bought this machine with a 5 ft cut which soon became capable of successfully handling over 100 types of crop. Credit for this really advanced product must go to Harry Merritt who, upon seeing the prototype demonstrated by its

originator, Bob Fleming, bought it in 1933. With the expertise of men such as John Mainland at La Porte, it was to become an outstanding commercial success within two years. Its production life exceeded 20 years, and in the UK, where it had become the first product at the new Essendine facility in 1951, many were still hard at work in the 1970s, with some working until quite recently in specialist applications. When supplied as an engine-driven type, the 60 power-unit version of the B engine was used with chaff screens and extended stacks—this engine also became available for the Roto-Baler, Forage Harvesters and Blowers. In later years, enlarged models were the 66, 72 and 90.

The Model A produced between 1936–41 was a combination of the K engine matched to a modified U rear end, and although not produced in significant numbers, it was a popular tractor as a four-plough machine, with up to 70 bhp from the $5\frac{1}{4}$ in. bore version. Other capabilities included 20 ft combines and 32 in. grain threshers, a speed of 10 mph and all-up weight of 7200 lb. Many of the 1200 built worked in the Dakotas, but they also gave good service in many other parts of the world. Here we see Carlos Antonio Peratta and son Xavier looking pleased with their nicely-restored Model A. Carlos also has a U, and he and I trade letters quite often on the subject of Allis-Chalmers. Hopefully, he will later be able to tell of other A-C tractors in and around his home in Cordoba, Argentina.

Not everyone needed a rowcrop-type tractor, so in order to provide greater market coverage the WF was introduced in 1937 as a basic version of the WC. This was mechanically similar but did not take the styled look until 1940, remaining in production for approximately 14 years in basic or industrial form, with a total of 8000 produced. This example belongs to Jim Crowe of Plainsville, Indiana.

Merritt and Roberts made a study of the tractor market and they 'got it in one'—their correct assessment found that the small farmer was not being catered for, which resulted in the appearance of the Model B in 1937 with Waukesha L-head engine for evaluation purposes, and full production commenced in 1938 with its own 16 hp V1H engine. With 11,703 built in 1938 alone, it was indeed a 'successor to the horse' and the 'hayburners' were on the way out as far as serious farm work was concerned. During its 19-year lifespan numerous improvements were made, with fully-adjustable front axle from 1940, foot brakes from 1941, 3⅜ in. bore from 1944, and so on. Mid-mounted mower, tool frames, and one- or two-way plough gave the 50-acre-plus farmer the right tools at the right price. An All-Crop 40 (inch) harvester was developed to suit, but owing to more pressing needs was dropped in 1942. Later sales advertisements featured it hauling the 60-engine-driven harvester. Also available from 1946 was the IB industrial, which was very handy for public-utility and golf-course work, to name but a few tasks.

The year 1938 was a busy one for Allis-Chalmers. However, the introduction of the Model S with 200-hour track-roller lubrication, plus restyling of the WC and development work at La Porte, did not affect the growth of the company, following the acquisition of the Brenneis Company of Oxnard, California. This company became yet another division of A-C and was particularly useful, specializing in deep-tillage equipment suitable for arid regions like the West Coast. The All-Crop 40 was designed and built with the B in mind. Keith White of Crediton, Devon, is the owner of this very rare UK-based machine.

Maybe they ran short of WC engines, but most
probably it was designed as a utility model—the
1939 RC was a combination of a WC frame with a
B/C engine. Around 5500 were built over a two-year
period, but a lacklustre performance, and economics,
soon caused it to yield to the Model C.

The year 1940 was a busy time for most manufacturers, but the HD 7, 10 and 14 series crawler tractors were an instant success. Power came from three-, four- and six-cylinder General Motors two-cycle diesels of 54, 79 and 108 hp, with the 14 being used for trials with torque-converter drive. When announced in 1947, the HD 19 was the largest of its type and the first with this kind of transmission—one of the many A-C innovations. Here we see the HD 14.

The Model B was a fine one-row tractor but many farmers needed that little bit extra, so the B was modified with a widespread rear end and tricycle-type or wide front axle, while the $3\frac{1}{4}$ in. bore was replaced by $3\frac{3}{8}$ in., with a $3\frac{1}{2}$ in. stroke, plus an additional 100 rpm to 1500 rpm for added power to work two-row

equipment. From 1940, a ten-year production life gave a total of 84,030 units, thus proving the wisdom of adding this model, known as the C, to the range. It is seen here with a two-row disc plough ideal for the heavier soils.

Above Worthy of mention is the M 7 Willys/A-C Northern Territories snow tractor for rescue operations. This M 7 is owned by Clell G. Ballard of Fairfield, Idaho, who puts it to good use in the winter.

Right A nicely-restored HD 5—part of the Parlour fleet of County Durham where, although finished to a very high standard, the machines still go out to work on the family's 350-acre arable farm when needed. Andrew Parlour will be only too pleased to show visitors his tractors, but please call him first as they are busy folk. The HD 5 and 5G loader variant appeared in 1946 as replacements for the M, and used the GM two-cycle, two-cylinder engines of 40.26 bhp. The 'G' designation applied to the loader variant of the Tractomotive Company of Deerfield, Illinois, who also offered a range of attachments, including a trencher (backhoe) attached to the loader arms—this company was absorbed into the Construction Equipment Division in 1959.

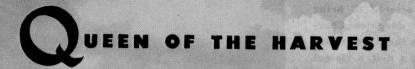

QUEEN OF THE HARVEST

SCOUR KLEEN
Gets the Weed Seeds

STRAW SPREADER
Scatters Straw Evenly

STRAW WINDROWER
Makes Straw-Saving Easy

Quietly and efficiently, the All-Crop Harvester has won its place in the hearts of farm families as the queen of harvesting machines. Well they know, it was the All-Crop Harvester that ended the weariness of shocking and threshing, and taught the new system of home harvesting.

When the nation's store of legume and grass seeds dwindled and threatened our food supply, it was the All-Crop Harvester that led the way. Millions of bushels harvested in the emergency are even now providing lush green forage for livestock and shielding bare soil.

A wide range of attachments increases the All-Crop Harvester's usefulness and versatility in handling over 100 different crops. Your dealer can show you how these attachments operate, among them a Scour-Kleen that removes dockage and weed seeds; a straw windrower that combines two swaths in one windrow so that the straw may be saved readily; and a straw spreader that scatters straw back on the land evenly...making it easy to plow under for soil-building.

Back of every sweetly humming All-Crop Harvester in the conscientious service of an Allis-Chalmers dealer whose motto is: "Long live the queen!"

TO BETTER LIVING
TO BETTER FARMING
TO MORE PROFIT

ALLIS·CHALMERS
TRACTOR DIVISION · MILWAUKEE 1, U. S. A.
ALL-CROP HARVESTER
"Successor to the Binder"

A March 1946 advertisement for the All-Crop Harvester—Queen of the harvest.

The G truck-farm/market-garden tractor, built at the Gadsden plant in Alabama, utilized a Continental AN 62 cu. in. engine, three fwd/one rwd plus special low, and a weight of 1400 lb. The French-built model was known as the GR and an old-time A-C man informed me that some of these were fitted with front-mounted engines; since this machine was originally designed for optimum visibility and clearance for the type of work required, I fail to see the logic behind this conversion. In typical Essendine fashion, a few were brought into the UK, without any apparent effort regarding marketing, with the result that another major company took up the basic design and marketed an improved version.

A large number of today's highly mechanized farms use a 'Big Roller' round baler, and although these appear to have mushroomed in popularity in recent years, the idea in fact goes back almost to the turn of the century. Thus, when A-C acquired the rights to the round baler from the Luebens family in 1939, a new name entered the farmer's vocabulary: Roto-Baler. The year 1947 saw the launch of this revolutionary machine, with the first UK trials taking place at Credenhill near Hereford, close to the temporary A-C base at Abbey Dore, and it was later displayed at the Royal Show in Lincoln. Advantages attributed to this method of baling included the fact that round bales gave a better finished product as opposed to the compression method of the square baler, and good weather-resistant characteristics meant that bales could be hauled in at the farmer's leisure. On the debit side, lack of dual-clutch tractors to cope with the stop/start operation and stacking problems meant that farmers turned to the rapidly-improving conventional balers with their continuous output and ease of handling. A Mk 10 automatic model appeared in 1958 but did not reach the UK.

Following an absence of five years, the B reappeared in the UK, initially assembled at the Totton plant near Southampton, but gradually locally-sourced components were bought in until, in its final form, it was totally UK-built at Essendine, Leicestershire. Supply companies included Bean Industries for castings, Rubery Owen for sheet metal, and Moss or ENV for transmissions, etc. The addition of hydraulics, four-speed transmission and Perkins P3 diesel option were notable improvements, but it was starting to show its age, and in 1955 it was replaced by the D 270. Several enterprising dealers carried out modifications to suit their customers' requirements—the above photograph shows a high-clearance model owned by Mr J. Willis of Essex. Ernest Doe Limited, who were well-known dealers, adapted several for orchard work by reducing the height and fitting fairings over the wheels; another enterprising farmer adapted a surplus tractor to carry quite a large number of irrigation pipes—the article quoting this feat makes no mention of stability problems or of 'tunnel-vision' visibility suffered by the driver!

By 1948 the WC was becoming rather long in the tooth owing to the growing need for hydraulic power lifts, and so the WD (seen here) was unveiled in 1948 at the same time as the G. Along with the hydraulics came two clutch-control and power-adjustable rear wheels (another A-C first). It is all too easy to be wise after the event, but this tractor would have maintained the good name the company held in the UK at this time, not to mention its ability to handle the Roto-Baler. The engine was as the WC, but this was obviously a tractor in keeping with its time, built from 1948–53.

By this time, the U, although only produced in relatively low numbers, had earned itself a fine reputation for power performance and reliability second to none, but time had overtaken it (though nothing else could). Since the UMA engine of $4\frac{1}{2}$ in. bore had been installed in 1936, along with full-width fenders and revised steering position, only minor modifications had been necessary, such was the proven design and quality of build.

Although the WF was also starting to run out of steam, it was to remain in use for quite some while yet. This WF-based loader was supplied by the Tractomotive Company and was very useful on farms and operations with bulk crops to handle. While in the ownership of Bert Schoo, it received a WD 45 engine for that extra power.

From 1919, the state of Nebraska decreed that all tractors sold in that state must be tested by the University of Nebraska Engineering Department for accuracy of performance claimed. The popularity and value of these tests to tractor manufacturers has come to mean that tractor companies worldwide now utilize this valuable facility. For details of tractors tested since 1950, the *Implement & Tractor* 'Red Book' gives comprehensive details of tests and results, as does the popular *Farm Tractors 1950–1975* by the ex-engineer in charge of the test laboratory, Lester Larsen. The figures show the month and year of the test, gas—gasoline, dis—distillate, and W—wide-tread.

Here is a summary of A-C tractors tested at Nebraska until 1950:

Test No.	Model	Month	Year	Test No.	Model	Month	Year
54	6-12	August	1920	302	B	May	1938
55	18-30	August	1920	303	WC	May	1938
56	18-30 (Monarch)	August	1920	304	WC gas	June	1938
82	12-12	September	1921	316	RC dis	April	1939
83	18-30	September	1921	336	WK	November	1939
151	30-35	June	1928	337	WS	November	1939
170	United (U)	November	1929	338	L	November	1939
189	All-Crop	April	1931	360	HD 7W	October	1940
193	EK	June	1931	361	HD 10W	October	1940
200	L	April	1932	362	HD 14	October	1940
215	Special K	September	1933	363	C dis	October	1940
216	M	September	1933	364	C gas	October	1940
223	W	May	1934	396	HD 5B	July	1948
237	U	July	1935	397	HD 19H	July	1948
238	UC	July	1935	398	G	July	1948
239	M	August	1935	399	WD dis	July	1948
285	WK O	August	1937	439	B	May	1950
286	S O	September	1937	440	WD gas	May	1950
287	L O	September	1937				

1. *Tailings elevator tensioner.*
2. *Rubber-faced beater bar.*
3. *Rubber-faced shelling plate.*
4. *Grain elevator tensioner.*
5. *Tailings return chute to drum.*
6. *Header drive belt.*
7. *Upper feed canvas.*
8. *Sack holder.*
9. *Lower feed canvas.*
10. *Reel height adjustment cord.*
11. *Header balance spring tension adjustment.*
12. *Header lift lever.*
13. *Header adjustment screw.*
14. *Engine oil filler.*
15. *Fuel fillers.*
16. *Engine oil level dipstick.*
17. *Engine oil filter.*
18. *Engine speed control.*
19. *Engine clutch.*
20. *Reduction gearbox oil filler.*
21. *Lower canvas tensioner.*
22. *Reel drive belt.*
23. *Header balance spring.*
24. *Drum drive pulley.*
25. *Sack discharge chute.*
26. *Gearbox control lever.*
27. *Gearbox oil filler.*
28. *Reel drive chain.*
29. *Grain elevator drive chain.*
30. *Drum drive adjustable tensioner.*
31. *Separator drive shaft.*
32. *Grain auger.*
33. *Tailings auger.*
34. *Sieve adjustment.*
35. *Chaffer adjustment.*
36. *Finishing sieve.*
37. *Wind valves.*
38. *Drum drive belt.*
39. *Grain drag.*
40. *Fan.*
41. *Tailings return chute to cleaning shoe.*
42. *Tailings return sieve.*
43. *Header adjustable tensioner.*
44. *Straw rack.*
45. *Straw deflectors.*
46. *Separator driving belt.*
47. *Adjustable chaffer.*
48. *Adjustable sieve.*
49. *Separator drive pulley (check speed here).*
50. *Slip clutch.*
51. *Wind valve control levers.*
52. *Grain drag adjustment.*
53. *Drum speed control.*

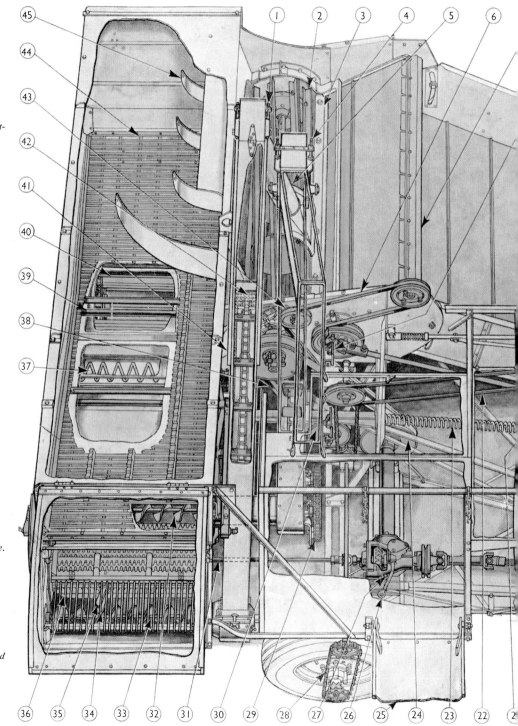

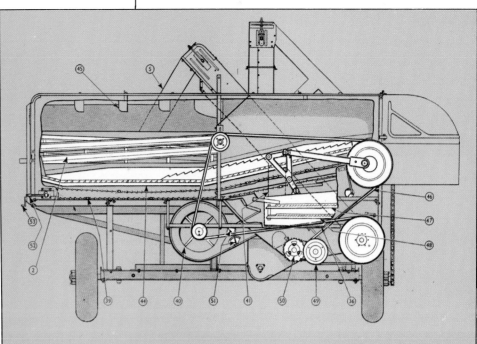

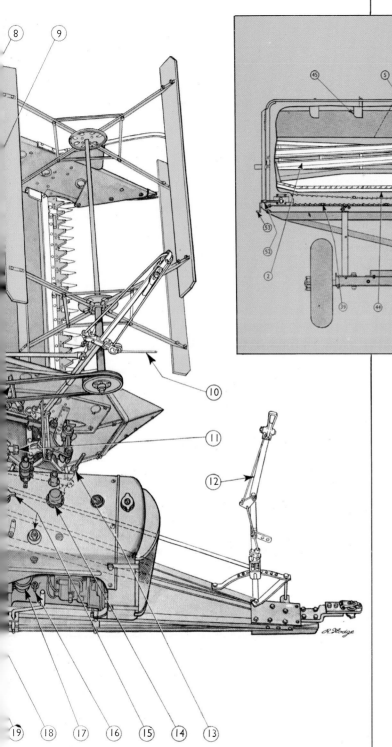

A cutaway drawing of the UK-built All-Crop 60 harvester.

The Model C was a good tractor, but developments taking place with other manufacturers meant that, in terms of power, traction and hydraulics, upgrading was necessary to keep pace. The CA (**above**), built between 1950–57, involved the fitting of power-adjustable rear wheels, 'Traction Booster' hydraulic control with the 'Snap Coupler' quick-hitch system (an A-C innovation), hand-operated transmission clutch giving a 'live-drive' facility, plus engine revs up to 1650 rpm, giving 26 hp—all of which made a good tractor even better.

The Ever Ready Company are famous for their batteries and electrical products, so it may have caused a few eyebrows to be raised when visiting their Watford factory to find a Roto-Baler installed for the purpose of baling waste paper. Modified with electric power and suitable safety screens, it proved to be an ideal machine for this task for a number of years.

Above One of the lesser-known products designed at La Porte, Indiana, was the 'Reaper Swather', which was intended to precede the harvesters in areas of high weed infestation or where wind and storm damage could affect ripened crops.

Right Roadless Traction Limited announce a half-track conversion for the Model B, this version having skeleton pads.

THE
ROADLESS NEWS

A JOURNAL OF INTEREST TO
THOSE WHO ARE CONCERNED
WITH TRANSPORT OVER
GROUND OF ALL DESCRIPTIONS.

Tel. Address "ROADLESS, HOUNSLOW."

Regd. Trade Mark
ROADLESS

Edited and Published Bi-Monthly by
ROADLESS TRACTION LIMITED,
GUNNERSBURY HOUSE, HOUNSLOW,
MIDDLESEX,   ENGLAND
Telephone : HOUNSLOW 6421.

Price 3d. (post free)

Vol. XVI. No. 1.

JANUARY — FEBRUARY 1952

THE ALLIS CHALMERS MODEL "B" WITH ROADLESS EQUIPMENT

THE Allis Chalmers Model " B " tractor fitted with Roadless Half Track Equipment makes an ideal tractor for the market gardener and the smaller farmer. The ruts made by a conventional wheeled tractor when working on a well prepared seed bed and which are so unwelcome are entirely eliminated by using the Skeleton type tracks. For the final preparation of a seed bed, for drilling, transplanting and for inter-row cultivation, the Allis Chalmers Model " B " fitted with Roadless Half Tracks is admirably suitable.

In very difficult conditions on the softest of seed beds, sustained drawbar pulls of upwards of 2,000 lbs. are readily obtainable and in firmer soil conditions, the drawbar pull can go up to as high as 3,000 lbs. The normal speeds of the machine fitted with pneumatic tyres remain virtually unaltered when the Half Tracks are fitted.

The price of the Equipment is £218 0s. 0d. ex works and it is distributed exclusively through Allis Chalmers accredited agents in both the home and overseas markets.

Fig. 1.—The Allis-Chalmers Model " B " fitted with Roadless Half Track Equipment and Skeleton Tracks at work hauling a 6 row trans-planter. The seed bed on which the outfit is working had previously been ploughed to a depth of 12 ins.; it was very light and it was only with the aid of the Half Tracks that the work was completed satisfactorily and without delay.

The first self-propelled harvester from Allis-Chalmers, although under development since 1947, did not become available until 1953. This All-Crop 100 is powered by the WD tractor engine, with a 9 ft header plus optional 3 ft extension, bagging unit, window pick-up and rotary flail-type straw spreader being optional extras. With the Gleaner-Baldwin Company soon to join the Agricultural Division in 1954, it had a short sales life.

Above November 1953 was important in the history of the company, the reason being that the well-known Buda Company, based in the Chicago suburb of Harvey, became the Engine & Lift Truck Division of A-C at that time. The growing lift-truck market would eventually be catered for by a separate division, but the immediate prize was their engine-building expertise and capacity. Buda had been building diesels since 1926 and from the late 1930s had offered conversions for Ford and IH trucks, with others later installed in tanks and aeroplanes (fancy a mid-winter flight in a diesel-powered Stinson Reliant?). Their total range, which included gasoline and LPG models, covered a wide range of hp ratings and applications, including the WD 45. The first diesel used a six-cylinder engine of 230 cu. in., developing 43.29 hp—this model and the gasoline/LPG options were produced from 1953–57 with the usual three- or four-wheel options. This photograph is of Bert Schoo's WD 45.

Right Following the Gleaner-Baldwin takeover in December 1954, A-C were quick off the mark to promote the products of this company from Independence, Missouri. Here we see a Model A 2 Gleaner combine, with 13 ft header, harvesting soybeans in Indiana.

A trial machine arrived in the UK in 1956 and, in spite of meeting adverse conditions, its success was such that a further 40 machines were sent in 1957 for European/UK evaluation trials. Of these, 20 were allocated to the UK market, and Les Dessurne of Newark, Nottinghamshire, still operates his machine alongside his 1960 HD 6B and a recently-restored HD 11 crawler, plus other B tractors. UK-built machines came off the line in 1958, with the first one destined for Portugal, while the first home sale was by Drake & Fletcher Limited of Ashford, Kent. Perkins P6 diesel or Austin-Newage gasoline/kerosene options, plus tanker or bagger options, were the main features.

Above Over the years, enterprising dealers and their customers have turned out some unusual but effective adaptations of existing machinery, such as the All-Crop 40 trailed machine, which was converted to be self-propelled for use in trial plot work at the National Institute of Agricultural Botany, based at Cambridge in the UK. The first conversion, though, was by the National Institute of Agricultural Engineering, of Silsoe, Bedfordshire, in 1954. This was followed by four others in 1955 from E. Allman & Company Limited, who were well-known, long-time A-C dealers. Until quite recently, several All-Crop 60s were also used by the NIAB. From the same area, A. T. Oliver & Company, agricultural engineers, were also innovative with their conversion of several tricycle-type tractors, including Model WCs, into sports-field rollers.

Right Gleaners in Norfolk, supplied by Cowlishaw & Son Limited. This company, along with the late John L. C. Flew of Broad Clyst, Devon, were of the old school—they went out and sold their products and followed up with good aftersales service.

Allis-Chalmers D-270 Tractor

KEY

A SNAP LINKS.
B HYDRAULIC PUMP.
C P.T.O. CONTROL.
D HYDRAULIC PUMP CONTROL.
E SNAP COUPLING RELEASE.
F AUXILIARY HAND CLUTCH.
G TOOL BAR AND ENGINE SIDE
　　WEIGHT ATTACHMENT POINTS.
H SNAP COUPLER
I INTERCHANGEABLE HITCH.

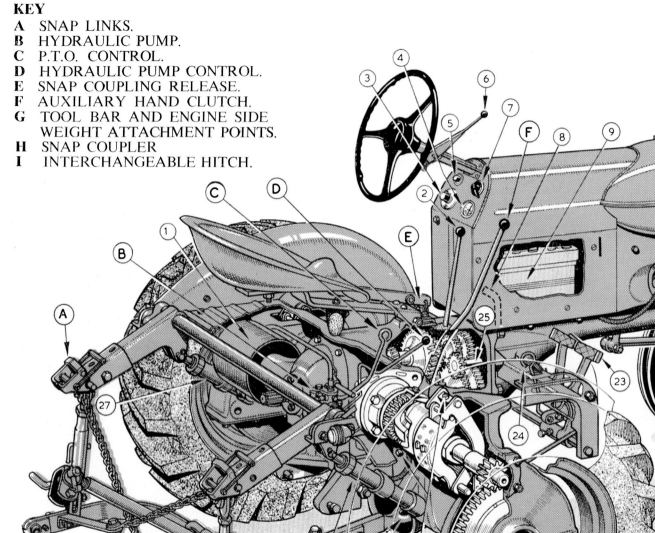

R. M. ELLIS

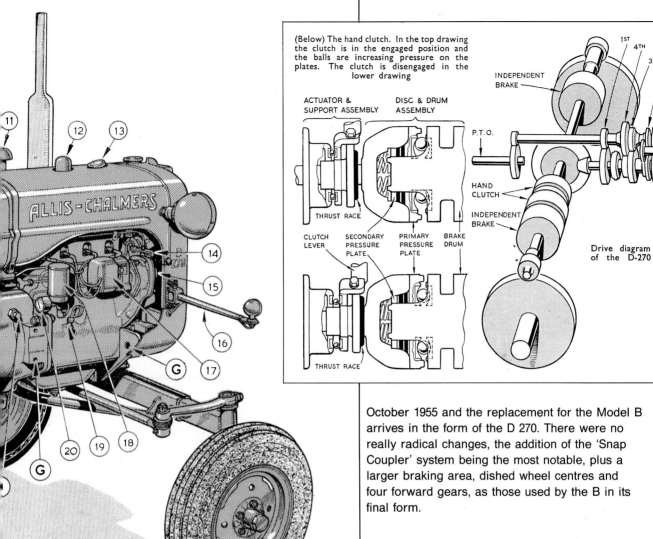

(Below) The hand clutch. In the top drawing the clutch is in the engaged position and the balls are increasing pressure on the plates. The clutch is disengaged in the lower drawing

ACTUATOR & SUPPORT ASSEMBLY

DISC & DRUM ASSEMBLY

THRUST RACE

CLUTCH LEVER

SECONDARY PRESSURE PLATE

PRIMARY PRESSURE PLATE

BRAKE DRUM

THRUST RACE

INDEPENDENT BRAKE

1ST 4TH 3RD REV. 2ND

P.T.O.

HAND CLUTCH

INDEPENDENT BRAKE

Drive diagram of the D-270

October 1955 and the replacement for the Model B arrives in the form of the D 270. There were no really radical changes, the addition of the 'Snap Coupler' system being the most notable, plus a larger braking area, dished wheel centres and four forward gears, as those used by the B in its final form.

ulley
ear lever
arter button
mmeter
ut out
and Throttle
ghts
lutch (Far side)
attery
el tank filler

11 Air cleaner intake
12 Oil filter and breather cap
13 Water temp. gauge
14 Throttle linkage
15 Engine governor
16 Retractable side lamp
17 Magneto
18 Oil filter
19 Dip stick
20 Oil pressure gauge

21 Starter motor locating screw
22 Starter motor
23 Independent brakes
24 Parking brake control
25 Four speed and reverse gear box
26 Brake adjustments
27 Hydraulic rams

The D 17 offered a four-cylinder 226 cu. in. 'Power Crater' engine in gasoline or LPG form, or the six-cylinder 262 cu. in. diesel of 51.14 belt hp. The D 17 shown here with the two-row Cotton Picker is owned by Salopek Bros. of La Cruces, New Mexico—the picture was taken on 21 October 1958 by Herb Zeck. With the end of B and C production at this time, no small tractors were offered until the D 10/12 of 1959 came along.

The year 1957 saw the end of the familiar styling that dated back to 1938, and the first tractors to appear in the new styling were the D 14 (three-plough) and D 17 (four- and five-plough) models. The D 14's features included a four-cylinder, 149 cu. in., 35 hp 'Power Crater' engine (there was no diesel option), a new selector for the 'Traction Booster' system, a 'Power Director' shift on the go-transmission (the big stick), a roll-shift front axle, a power-shift rear-wheel track, and much more. This example belongs to the Goselink family of the Netherlands.

Essendine also introduced a new model—out went the 'chubby B' (D 270) and in came the D 272. There was still nothing dramatic by way of change, but it became quite popular. Its features included a squared-off styling, dual throttle settings for gasoline/kerosene use, Perkins P3-144 as used in later 270s, and an unusual three-point hitch that gave an option of hooking the top link to a cross-tube between the lower arms, with the claimed advantage of giving the flexibility of trailed implements as well as the mounted. The high-clearance model is seen here outside the showroom of Cowlishaw & Son Limited, of Methwold, Norfolk, well-known A-C dealers since 1933, their first sale being a Model U on 9 October 1933. Standard and low models were also available.

Above A 19th-century idea becomes something of a
radically new concept for farm power in 1959—
another example of A-C's research and development
policy. The fuel-cell tractor was just one of their
many projects at this time, which would also include
spot welders and lift trucks using this power; a
healthy involvement in NASA space projects was
also in progress at the same time. Utilizing a basic D
10/12, the 1008 fuel cells were fed a mixture of gases
and oxygen, with the resulting power being fed
through a 20 hp DC motor and controller, giving
3000 lb tractive effort at a weight of 5270 lb. This
tractor now resides at the Museum of American
History (Smithsonian Institute).

Small tractors reappeared with the D 10/12. For one- or two-row operations, the D 10 was a popular tractor favoured by small farmers, though a little costly for the time. Here is a 139 cu. in., 34 hp D 10 with a two-spool hydraulic system, 'Snap Coupler' hitch and drawbar, low-clearance muffler, and equipped with a No. 110 cultivator and side-dressing attachment, cultivating tobacco while on demonstration by Wyatt Farm Machinery Company, South Boston, Virginia, at W. T. Covington's farm.

New products for 1960 included the D 15 (to replace the D 14), and the H 3 gasoline/HD 3 diesel crawler tractors, which had either the 139 cu. in. engine or the 175 cu. in. diesel of 40 hp. The shuttle clutch or 'Power Director' transmission with live pto and three-point hitch were for the farmer, while the 1066 loader and 1003 scarifier were for the contractor. This is another nice example from the Parlour fleet—this base machine is quite rare in the UK as most of the models on this side of the Atlantic were of the loader variety.

Above Last of the UK models was the diesel-only ED 40 of 1960. A Standard Ricardo 2.3-litre engine provided 37 hp at 2000 rpm, while from July 1963 2250 rpm gave 41 hp and a new (rather naughty) 'Depthomatic' hydraulic system was adopted. This was a tractor you either loved or hated, depending on whether you had this particular system or the easier selective weight-transfer type. This tractor was photographed in Canada with a No. 14 plough.

Overleaf D 15 tractor with fork-lift attachment.

Takeover time again—A-C take a controlling interest in *Establiscoments de Construction Mécaniques de Vendeuvre SA*, usually referred to as *Vendeuvre*. With headquarters in Paris and the main plant in Dieppe, their principal products were air-cooled diesel tractors, industrial engines and generators. Road graders and lift trucks would become main products, with the emphasis on the latter after 1968 when the European Handling Division was formed. The tractors (**left**) are pictured at the time of A-C's initial involvement—the later FD 3/4/5 series would show the inherent US styling of the D series, as did the ED 40, also offered in France with the D 17. The above illustration is of a rather rusty FD 3, approximately 20 miles north of Nantes.

The tractor range for 1961 was extended with the addition of the D 19, powered by the G 262 gasoline/LPG engine of 71–76 hp or the D 262T diesel of 66.92 hp maximum. This was the first tractor tested at Nebraska in turbocharged form, and is seen here in 'Beachmaster' guise, along with its 'Beach Sanitizer' unit—a high-capacity combination for cleaning large areas of pleasure beaches.

Above A licensing agreement took place between A-C and Jones Balers Limited of Mold, Clwyd, makers of conventional pick-up balers and manure spreaders, etc, to build 10,000 balers in the US over a five-year period. Glyn and David Jones saw the A-C diamond erected on their Mold and Rhosesmor plants in September 1961, and the original Star and Super Star balers became the 200/300 series as A-C products. Other products to follow would include the 77 side-rake/tedder, 157 and 214 drills and hay conditioners. The Mold factory also became a support plant for the Essendine facility.

Right Producing low-volume specialist machinery is often a financial 'no-go area', but adaptations of existing products can often cover that particular sector and provide the desired results with the minimal disruption to design work or factory routine. This T 16 four-wheel-drive cane tractor is a typical example. Based on the TL 16 loader, with seat and driving position reversed and with some sheet-metal modifications, it would prove to be a much more cost-effective venture; its engine was the 7000-series, turbocharged 135 hp (later 150 hp) diesel from the Harvey works. The original idea is thought to have originated at the plant in Springfield, Illinois, which is now owned by Fiat/Allis North America Inc.

Above David and Goliath, or the world's largest bulldozer at the time of its announcement at the Chicago Roadshow in 1963. The HD 41 is shown alongside the B 1 garden tractor, which was produced for Allis-Chalmers by the Simplicity Manufacturing Company of nearby Port Washington, who in 1965 were to join the company.

Right Increased production and bigger farms meant bigger tractors were needed, and on 6 July 1963 the largest tractor to emerge from West Allis was announced as the D 21, the first 100 hp for farm use. Its all-up weight was almost 7 tons, and its D 3400 engine gave 107 hp through an 8F/2R transmission. From 1965, the D 21 (series II) put out 127 hp from a D 3500 turbocharged engine, and hydrostatic front-wheel assist became optional. As well as its seven-plough rating, advertising quoted it as being capable of operating four-wheel hydraulic pan scrapers.

616 Cotton Picker at work on the Grady Johnson farm, owned by J. J. Webb of Twin City, Georgia.

D 17 (series IV) with No. 505 six-row planter and pre-emerge spray, planting at the company sales farm at Racine, South Milwaukee.

A 1973 Model MH Gleaner hillside combine at work on the Fred McNeally & Sons farm at Colfax, Washington, as a demonstrator from the Independence works.

Left The year 1964 saw a new styling for the tractor range on the new 190 and 190 XT (turbo), followed by the 160 (later 6040), 170, 175, 180, 185, 200, 210 and 220 models which were produced over the next decade, details of which can be seen in the 'Red Book' mentioned earlier. The 190 used the well-proven 301 cu. in. engine at 77 hp in basic form and the usual gasoline/LPG options were also available. Twelve-position seating and cane or rice models were additions to the normal extras or options. The picture shows a 190 TX (series III), with a four-row 'No-Til' planter, double-cropping corn in wheat stubble in Kentucky.

Above The Henry Manufacturing Company of Topeka, Kansas, were big suppliers of loader and other attachments to A-C, and were in fact to join the company in 1968 as the Industrial Tractor Division. Shown here is an I 40 industrial tractor at work, in the ownership of Kenneth Royer of Oak Grove, Missouri. Other attachments were also available from Shawnee, Wagner, Howard and others.

For the heavier tillage work, the HD 16 fits the bill perfectly, with around 150 hp and a weight of 31,500 lb. Here we see Anderson-Clayton Farms subsoiling in California with Brenneis equipment.

An HD 4 farm crawler tractor at work on the Racine sales farm. It had a 200 cu. in., 59 hp gasoline or 52 hp diesel engine, with 3-3 shuttle-clutch reverse-mounted radiator, and dozer, loader, winch or scarifier options.

The 160 built by Renault of France to A-C
specifications has the Perkins 3.152 40.36 hp engine
and is the replacement for the D 15. It is shown here
with roll-bar canopy and 390 mower-conditioner.

An early offering from the newly-formed Industrial Tractor Division. The 'Buckmaster' pulpwoods-lasher/loader (**above**) was an ideal machine for the farmer or custom operator with any volume of lumber to handle. The 160 cu. in. gasoline or 200 cu. in. diesel engine with foot-operated shuttle reverser, 14 ft lift, 21 forward and nine rearward tilt, side shift, 48 in. disc and other options, including a radio, made this a one-man type of operation. Illustrated left are a trio of 714/715 loaders and backhoe/loader units on display at the Topeka facility. Other more recent products include small four-wheel-drive loaders and tractor-mounted fork lifts.

Since 1960, Essendine had placed strong emphasis on the production of the TL loader range, which later became the 345-945 range of pivot-steer models, and farm equipment began to lose favour in the late 1960s owing to the increase in loader production. The 5000 combine of 1969 was the last new product to appear, but with such a low demand for farm equipment, this resulted, in 1971, in the sale of A-C farm-machinery rights and plants in the UK to what is now known as the Bamford International Company of Uttoxeter, Staffordshire. They continued operating the Mold facility, while Essendine stayed in A-C ownership until 1 January 1974, when the joint Fiat/Allis agreement combined the construction equipment interests of these two famous names. The 5000 was discontinued at the time of the merger but balers and drills, etc, were available after this date, even after the closure of Mold and the subsequent transfer to Uttoxeter.

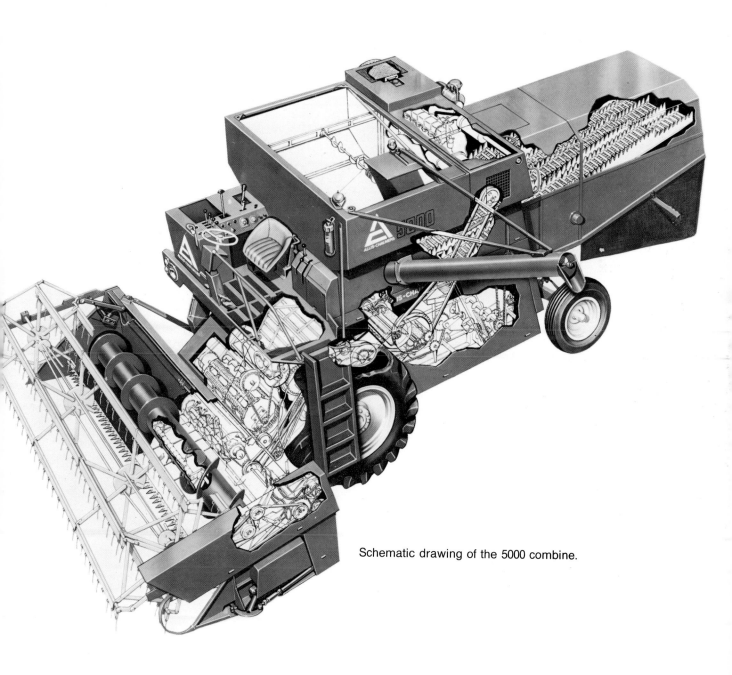

Schematic drawing of the 5000 combine.

New for 1970 were the 175 and 185 'Crop Hustler' tractors. The 175 offered the Perkins 4.248 direct-injection diesel engine of 62.47 pto hp or the final development of the 226 cu. in. 'Power Crater' engine, which first appeared with WD 45. A long production run exceeding ten years suggests that these were popular tractors. The 185, with the long-established 301 engine and a host of options, has, according to my contacts in the US, been held in very high regard. It is seen here with the 2300-series disc harrow.

The 170 of 1967–73, which offered the Perkins 4.236
engine or 226 cu. in. gasoline engine.

The year 1971 saw A-C retitled as the Allis-Chalmers Corporation, and in 1972 the first full four-wheel drive in A-C livery appeared. However, it was a custom-built exercise from the Steiger Tractor Company of Fargo, North Dakota, utilizing an 855 cu. in. V8 Cummins of 208 maximum hp, 10F/2R and 40 degrees articulation left or right. Approximately 1039 were built to 1975. This 440 was photographed in October 1971 and is seen at work, chisel-ploughing on test.

Line-up of Gleaner combines for the 'Proud Programme' 50th Anniversary presentation at Las Vegas, Nevada, in 1973. From left to right, the models date from 1960, 1951, 1926 and 1923.

The 720 Forager, with attachments.

The 200 with the new comfort cab. The specification was as for the 190 that it replaced.

Above In 1973, the farming media covered the country with a heavy-duty campaign telling the public that the 'Orange Age' had begun, the explanation for this being the introduction of a new range of tractors known as the 7000 series. First to appear were the 7030 and 7050 of 130 hp and 156 hp respectively, with the 7050 having the new intercooling system. The 'Power Squadron' would eventually cover the following models: 7000, 7010, 7020, 7040, 7045, 7060 and 7080. These incorporated 301 and 426 cu. in.

engines, various stages of turbocharging, counter-balanced crankshafts, piston coolant, plus 12-speed power shift or 20-speed 'Power Director' transmissions, easy-access panels and all refinements, with sound ratings down to 76 dB.

Right The original HD 6 of 1956 gave 63.99 belt hp from its 344 cu. in. engine, but later models were uprated to 80 hp. This was a popular machine for heavy-tillage operations.

Allis-Chalmers built attractive tractors, but they lost this contest! The 7580 of 1975 replaced the 440 and was the first high-performance tractor from West Allis. Power came from a Harvey-built 670 HI engine of 222 base hp and 426 cu. in. capacity, with a 20-speed 'Power Director' transmission, and the Acousta 11 cab gave a sound rating of 79 dB. The 8550 of 1978 used the 6120 engine of 305 base hp and 731 cu. in. capacity.

Above A-C and Deutz-Allis meet up in London—well, almost! These are recent Ertl issues of $\frac{1}{16}$th scale-model promotionals. Marketing farm machinery involves much more than glossy brochures on dealers' desks and parts counters. Promotional aids include items such as video tapes, slide and 16 mm film shows, and second-line products ranging from key fobs, pens, wearables, and a vast range of consumables up to main product support items such as the 'Terra Tiger' rough-terrain personal transport vehicles, all wearing the company logo.

Toy tractors and implements play an important part in projecting the company name, and Ron Eggan and fellow Missourian Glen Bridges are but two of the many collectors in this fast-growing leisure

pursuit. My own collection of A-C/Deutz-Allis and Deutz models now stands at over 60 items, and many thanks to Ron for his efforts on my behalf.

Right West Allis was a vast complex but a lot of other products took up a large part of its area, and with high design and tooling-up costs, the company opted, as did other major manufacturers, to utilize small/medium tractors built on high-production-capacity lines and finished off in the individual company liveries. Shown here is the 5040; the 5050 was a 50 hp model from Fiat, the 5040 was from UTB, and the compact 5015, 5020 and 5030 models were standard Far East-produced models, with A-C styling.

With the growth in popularity of minimum or no-tillage farming practice in the 1970s, A-C users were catered for with chisel ploughs, 'Min-Til' conservation tools, chiselvators and other related equipment.

The year 1978 saw the appearance of the N 5, 6 and 7 series of rotary combines from Independence. The innovative new layout involved the cylinder being mounted transversely, giving numerous design and operational advantages. Flexible headers to 24 ft and conventionals to 30 ft, grain-bin capacities to 315 bushels and other up-to-date features made it a machine for the progressive farmer. When equipped for corn harvesting, capacities went from four up to 12 rows. This range was complementary to the conventional L, M, K and MH hillside models. The latest development of the rotary harvester is the R 50, 60 and 70 range.

While enjoying a tour of the tractor plant in 1980, I saw two pilot models of the new 6060 and 6080 tractors on the line. These were to be replacements for the 175 and 185 that were now a little long in the tooth, and incorporated Fiat rear end with A-C Type 433 diesel in turbocharged form and intercooling for the 6080. Also on this visit I was lucky enough to see a 1160-ton, 43,200 shp ship's diesel being readied for a press release the next day—that, however, is another story. . . .

Another new model was announced in 1982—of 40 hp, 10/2R and with a comprehensive range of standard and optional equipment, it was a custom-built product, finished in A-C livery, and designated the 6140. This is the grassland model.

A-C unveiled a full range of new heavies at Reno, Nevada. All were 100 hp plus, with the actual rating corresponding to the last two digits: 8010, 8030, 8050 and 8070. They were all available with a front-wheel-assist option. At the same time, the 4W 220 and 305 models replaced the 7580/8550 tractors.

The wheel turns full circle! The Simplicity Manufacturing Company, having spent the past 20 years as the Lawn & Garden Equipment Division of A-C, are once again an independent company—but now they are supplying a new company at West Allis. Of course, their own brand name continues as before.

The last new model to be designed and built at West Allis was also the last to leave the line on 6 December 1985. A sad but sure fact of life is that nothing is forever, and the harsh trading conditions facing the farming world today has resulted in numerous vital reappraisals of production policies by nearly all the major companies in this industry. Consequently, the famous West Allis building, which had produced a very popular tractor range since 1914, closed for business on that day in December.

Following a positive appraisal of the farm-equipment market, both in the USA and worldwide, and bearing in mind the trading conditions which had caused several major tractor and implement companies to effect severe restructuring plans, including downsizing and product rationalization, the Allis-Chalmers Corporation and the Klöckner-Humboldt-Deutz AG group of Cologne, West Germany, agreed to a merger of both companies' farm-machinery interests from 24 May 1985. By combining the 124 years of innovative, high-grade expertise built up by A-C with the very considerable technical and financial strengths of KHD, a company of even greater international stature would emerge, better able to face the still-uncertain future of world farming today. KHD AG are now the owners of the Agricultural and Credit Divisions of Allis-Chalmers.

The photographs are of Bodo Liebe, Chairman of KHD (**above left**), and Manfred Hopf, Chairman of the Deutz-Allis Corporation (**above right**).

Nicolaus August Otto (**above**) was born the son of an innkeeper in Holzhausen, Germany, in 1832. Inspired by the much-publicized work of the French inventor Lenoir relating to the development of the gas engine, Otto in partnership with Eugen Langen from 1864 soon developed an atmospheric engine of more advanced design than before. The acclaim from the Paris Exhibition of 1867 led to the opening of a factory at Deutz, near Cologne, and 1872 saw the formation of the Gasmotoren-Fabrik Deutz AG, now KHD AG. The Otto 'silent' gas engine appeared in 1876, which was the world's first four-cycle engine, whose operating principle is still unchanged today. On his death on 22 January 1891, his legacy to industry, indeed to the world at large, was motive power in the truest sense, and he in turn became an inspiration to others, such as Gottlieb Daimler and Rudolph Diesel.

The original Otto four-cycle engine of 1876.

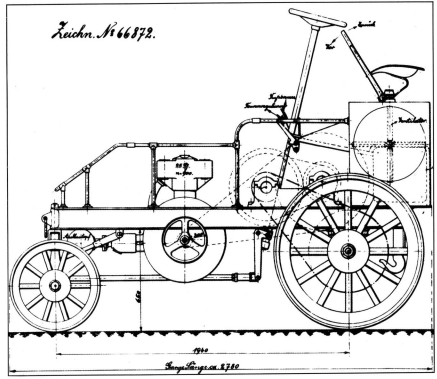

An 1894 tractor from the
'Otto-Gas-Engine-Works' in
Philadelphia (**above**),
accompanied by a design
for 1907 (**right**).

Zeichn. № 66872.

Early stationary-engine application in agriculture.

				1969	**WEDAG** Westfalia Dinnendahl Gröppel AG	
Motoren-Werke Mannheim AG	**1985**			**1959**	**Vereinigte Westdeutsche Waggonfabriken AG**	
Maschinenfabrik Fahr AG	**1968**				**van der Cypen und Charlier**	**Gebr. Gastell**
C. D. Magirus AG *	**1936**					**Gastell & Harig**
Motorenfabrik Oberursel AG	**1930**	**1930** Humboldt-Deutzmotoren AG		**1930**	**Maschinenbauanstalt Humboldt AG**	
Motorenfabrik Wilhelm Seck & Cie		**1921** Motorenfabrik Deutz AG			**Maschinenbau AG Humboldt**	
		1872 Gasmotoren-Fabrik Deutz AG			**Maschinenfabrik für den Bergbau von Sievers & Co.**	
		1869 Langen, Otto und Roosen				
		1864 N. A. Otto & Cie				

KHD

1938 Klöckner-Humboldt-Deutz Aktiengesellschaft

*In 1975 separated as Magirus-Deutz AG from the KHD group and incorporated in IVECO. In 1980, KHD shares in IVECO assigned to Fiat.

Outline of the build-up of the Klöckner-Humboldt-Deutz AG group of companies.

121

A new concept in farm power was the air-cooled diesel engine introduced by Deutz in 1950, the first tractor so equipped being the F1L 514 of 15 ps (hp). Since that time, 3.8 million units of various sizes have been built in Germany and France for a wide range of applications, with a further 0.7 million produced under licence.

The St Nicolaus event in 1986. Prominent in the above picture is a limited-edition model of 1970, with the famous 11 ps (hp) Bauernschlepper of the 1936–50 period beside it—this tractor had a parallel in the Model B in that it brought mechanization to the small farmer. In September 1987, I had great pleasure in attending the 'Oldtimer' event at Hanigsen, near Hanover. There, thanks to my pal Wilhelm Lange, I got to meet up with other old friends, such as Michael Bruse and Jorg Alvermann, and made many more. Although by usual standards not a large event, it was well stocked with a wide range of Deutz and other tractors which, added to the picturesque setting and friendly crowds, means that I will make a great effort to pay a return visit.

Back to square one, or rather circles. The old Luebens/A-C idea of round bales (**left**), aided by the passing of time and considerable development, has now become a key item on today's farming scene. The bales may be bigger but the basic principle is just the same. Shown above is a Simplicity/Deutz-Allis garden tractor.

Typical air-cooled engine for agricultural application.

On today's tractor, in the space following the word 'Deutz' on the cab will be written 'Fahr' if destined for the European market, or 'Allis' if for North America. While all current tractors are air-cooled, the Motoren-Werke Mannheim AG company, makers of liquid-cooled engines, were acquired at the time of the Deutz-Allis formation in 1985. Marketing conditions and policies can, at times, change rapidly, and currently under review is the option of a US-built tractor produced on an existing line, possibly in Ohio.